DANDELION

by Ladislav Svatos

Doubleday & Company, Inc.
Garden City, New York

for Alex,
the Big Boy,
and Andrew,
the Small One

ISBN: 0-385-02913-6 TRADE
        0-385-04629-4 PREBOUND
Library of Congress Catalog Card Number 73-20911
Copyright © 1976 by Ladislav Svatos
All Rights Reserved
Printed in the United States of America

9   8   7   6   5   4   3   2

Do you know
the dandelions?
They grow in lawns,
looking
like little suns
popping out of the grass.
And do you know
how the dandelions
grow up?
Let's look . . . . .

One day
the yellow flowers change
into fluffy balls
full of seeds.
It means
the plant is ready
to spread
new life
all around.

Each dandelion seed
has a little silvery soft parachute.
And the wind can take it
and carry it far away.

The seeds
will softly glide
down to earth.
They need the earth
to grow up
into a new plant.

The seeds also need water to grow.
The morning dew and the rain will help.

When it is moist,
the seed is ready
to grow up
into a new dandelion.
It begins
to spread out roots
and the first little leaves
start to show up.

The shining sun
will provide warmth,
which is so important
for most living things.

With the wind to carry it,
with the soil to hold it,
with the rain to moisten it,
and the sun to warm it,
the seed is fast growing
into a young plant.

The dandelion
is growing and growing,
spreading its leaves wide
and opening its buds
into rich sun-yellow flowers.

Each flower
has many yellow leaflets
called florets,
and each floret is actually
a single flower by itself.
Soon a new seed
will be formed
in almost every floret.

The flowers
start to wither away.
They close up,
the seeds develop
into little parachutes,
and when
they open up again
they have changed
into silky heads
full of seeds.

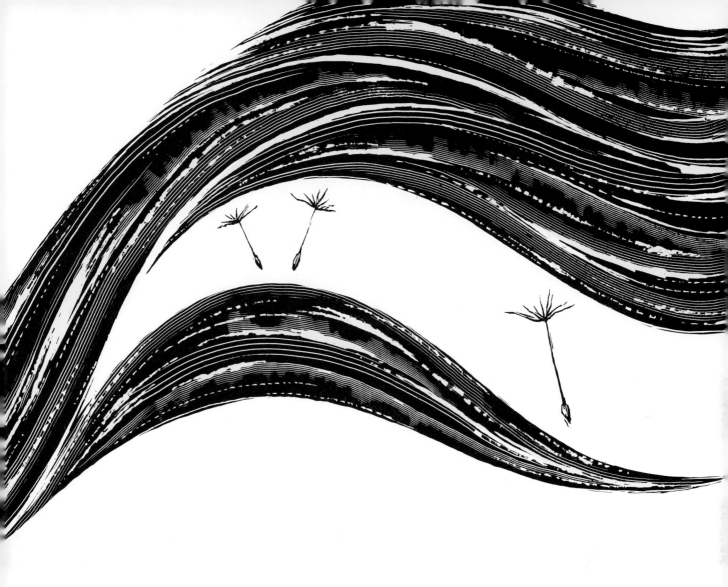

The wind comes
and the whole story of life
will start again.

Ladislav Svatos
was born and educated
in Czechoslovakia
and began his career
as an artist there.
Since coming to the United States,
he has worked as an art director,
designer and illustrator
and now is a free-lance artist,
working out of Connecticut
on books for all age levels.
He has won several awards
for his books
both in Europe and
in the United States,
including awards from the
American Institute of Graphic Arts
and the Art Directors Club
of New York.